THE PEARL INSIDE THE ORCHID

An Anthology of Poems by
Gaudys Laxury

The Pearl inside the Orchid

by Gaudys Laxury

THE PEARL INSIDE THE ORCHID
Copyright © 2015 by Gaudys Laxury

www.glaxarts.com
E–mail: glaxarts@gmail.com
Book and cover design by Jennifer Marie Decio
Copy Editor: Catherine Chen

Printed in the United States of America

ISBN 13: 978-0-9966733-2-7
First Edition: December 2015
10 9 8 7 6 5 4 3 2 1

TABLE OF CONTENTS

TABLE OF CONTENTS

DEDICATION

I dedicate this book to my mother and father, Rosa and Santiago Sanclemente for all the love, encouragement, and sacrifice. Thank you both for giving me strength to reach for the stars and chase my dreams. My sister, Zulma Youngs, for the love and support.

Special thanks to Eleni Mouzouris-Indjeyiannis, for always being there during my academic, professional and artistic endeavors—who encouraged me to paint and write—pushing me to enhance my creative juices and always supporting my aspirations.

This book would not have been possible without the help of an amazing creative team—Kitty Cat and Jen D., thank you wholeheartedly for making the process fun. Your friendship makes my life a wonderful experience.

As an act of love, I also dedicate this book to all of you who have inspired me. You know who you are—my beautiful muses!!

Throughout many stages of my life, I have written down words, sentences, random thoughts, feelings, and emotions. Similarly, my artworks derive from spontaneous inspirations. Collectively, words and art embody my heart and soul—art is universal.

The collections of poetry in this book are accompanied with originally created artworks. Some of the poems are written in Spanish, while most in English—but all designed to inspire, channel emotions, and connect readers on a deeper, spiritual, and inspirational level.

This book is a result of the impossibility, the push by family and friends to dream big and accomplish a bucket list of sorts. I never thought it was possible to publish these poems and artworks, but as rare as it is to find a pearl inside an orchid, with a little bit of imagination, perseverance, and faith—anything is possible.

"I am the master of my fate. I am the captain of my soul."
—William Ernest Henley

Inspirational

Gaudys Laxury
CLARIDAD **(2015)**
Oil on Canvas
12 x 24 inches

CLEAR AS OCEAN BLUE

Living life and seeking the truth,
while running like a wolf.
Finding out what we can do in this lifetime,
curious of the realm of things that are sublime.

Looking through the two-sided hourglass,
hoping that it will just one day pass.
Today we will find it, I say to you;
and one day it will all be clear as ocean blue.

To find out who we are and what we want to do,
crazy life, lousy life—it's like a taboo.
Walking through the misty gray air,
will not be where the answers lie as you walk there.

You come across a golden thing,
thinking it might just be your everything.
A stepping stone of opportunity,
taking it will lead you to infinity.

Seeking hopes and dreams—finding that muse,
one day it will come and it's no excuse.
Chatting and talking, just doing your thing,
singing and swaying, it's what life brings.

The answer you'll see in just about everything,
with open eyes and a smile it will bring.
Happiness you shall find for your questions in life,
will be accomplished for that which you strive.

FORWARD

All things are possible when faith is at hand;
all things are clear when you're in command.
Push onward and upward against all obstacles and fears;
keep your eyes wide open, heart beating, and
listen with your ears.

Positive thoughts, kept in the present,
negative directions are not so pleasant.
The harder you try, the good that will come,
the bruises you endure, the stronger you'll become.

One quick, loud blow to break the ice,
don't hold back, don't be so nice.
With one deep breath, exhale and yell;
release all frustrations and get out of your shell.

All things are possible when you're in control;
roll the dice, take a risk, and aim for your goal.
Two steps forward, no steps back;
dance if you have to, keep moving, and don't slack.

Long, deep breaths, flow with the currents of the sea;
sooner than you know it, at peace you'll be.

ROSE QUARTZ
Dedicated to Hun Wong, RIP

Treasure life and live each moment as if it were the last;
smile, one second each day—don't live in the past.
Hug and give yourself a pat;
live, dance, and be free—don't be a doormat.

But if no smiles come out,
then try a different route.
The path to live day by day and moment to moment,
the would, should, could—a time well spent.

Aim for your dreams to make it happen,
as life could pass you by;
avoid the dead ends, the blackouts, and pitfalls—just fly.

Life can stop without a moment's notice,
a grandfather clock that stands still;
but pause for a second and go, go, go—climb up that hill.

Don't wrap yourself in four walls without smelling the roses;
see life through a rose quartz—aim for positive choices.

ALGUN DÍA LLEGARAS

Un paso atrás y varios hacia delante;
una mirada a la izquierda y derecho—eso es bastante.

¡No espera!

Mira dentro de ti, nunca por afuera;
cuidado con esa mirada, sabemos lo que quisiera.
Y si miras hacia afuera, respira profundamente;
que siempre hay sombras esperando, pueda que sea la gente.

Dos pasos para tras, tres pasos para delante;
no camines como tortuga, ni león, ni un elefante.
Pero siempre corriendo para alcanzar la luz;
ni tampoco correr como moto, avión, ni autobús.

Despacio, despacio que algún día llegaras;
con respiro y paciencia en las manos lograras.

EMPIRE SKIES

Live your life and do what you want.
Listen to your inner self;
it does you no wrong.

    —freedom from all
    —freedom from the world
    —freedom from yourself
    —freedom from impossibilities

Open up your heart and feel what is real.
One look, one voice, one mind;
an infinite impact on others.
Be it realism, optimism, pessimism;
live your life and listen to your inner self.

The empire skies are up and above your reach,
and yet close enough to touch.

    —freedom from doubts
    —freedom from the conventional
    —freedom from the norm

Live your life beyond the empire skies.

FLY AND SOAR
Dedicated to Norka Collado, a beautiful bird

Sad news, bad news, harsh news—
brush away.

Transform into an eagle,
let the sickness stay at bay.
Fly like an eagle, drift swiftly in the air—

      Fly, fly.

Spread the wings; soar as high as the sky.
Fly past the sea, past the trees, past the roads and flatlands;
past the heartaches, pains, and woes—
cards that dealt bad hands.

Fly into the mountains, rest, meditate;
let the sickness pass you by.

Let the wings shed, claws fall—
this is not the moment to die.
A change is near, a transformation into the unknown.

Welcome new beginnings, a rebirth—
the eagle has flown.

GET UP AND GO!!!

Creating all these questions in our lives and
changes in our soul,
makes us think of who we are,
perhaps an empty hole.

So many obstacles to conquer,
hopefully one day to be fulfilled.
But until then we put on our shoes and get up and go—
not the moment to standstill.

Get up and go, get up and go, get up and go…
until the end of time.
Love yourself, live the life, seek the answers in your mind.

Get up and go until the end of time
and through it all we breathe just to listen to ourselves.
Become one with nature, one with ourselves,
one with all the obstacles that cross our paths.

One day we will be able to lie back and breathe;
and relax and think of all the things we have accomplished.

Believe in the things that will happen,
as they happen for a reason.
The time will come where all answers will have closure
and obstacles past season.

CASIO GUY

Riding the subway the other day,
in walks a young guy from out of the blue.
Decides to sit down on the ground and play a tune for us—
      who knew?

Didn't sing, didn't announce,
this calm fella—let's call him Joe.
Who very smoothly starts jamming away,
on his old school Casio.

The tune, I must say, was cool as the sea,
while people were reading, waiting,
drinking their coffees and tea.

An almost sadness to this Joe fella as I listened to his tune,
thinking about all the struggles in this economy—
      don't let it last 'til June.

But this Joe fella is a pure inspiration for us to admire,
at how he jammed away at his Casio—
      without a care and to inspire.

Kith & Kin

Gaudys Laxury
Eye See You (2013)
Oil on Canvas
16 x 20 inches

THE PEARL INSIDE THE ORCHID

New Horizons

The day is near for big decisions to be made;
it's like a chess game—one of which you've played.
New opportunities wait for you far and near;
so keep your eyes and ears open and your mind very clear.

Note that there are many bumps in the road, from time to time,
that put a bad taste in your mouth like a Spanish lime.
But always strive to be strong as a bull and fearless at time of war;
and able to tackle all obstacles like a Latin conquistador.

Whatever you decide in life,
whatever road is meant to be driven,
always know your friends and family will stand behind you—
that's a given.

TRIUNFADOR

Triumph is in the eye of the beholder.

Walking alone is like walking in vain;
but with great support and loyalty,
you'll meet your dreams—just aim.

But if walking alone, walk with determination and faith;
you are a Triunfador.
Alone or with family, push hard to succeed;
add some persistence—it's time to explore.

Climb up those steps, walk higher and higher,
with no end to your goal.
Climb up that mountain, aim for the sky—be bold.

Don't hold back, don't look behind, don't walk in reverse;
keep your eye on the prize.
Triumph is in the eye of the beholder;
be your own person, you are a Triunfador—be wise.

UN POEMA PARA LAS MADRES
Dedicado a mi madre, Rosa, la flor más bella de la ciudad.

Una persona única, especial, fundamental;
Que trae sonrisas y alegría—más allá del auroral.
Siempre apoyando sin pensar;
Nunca pensando de abandonar.
Es la gran persona de nuestras vidas;
La número uno, siempre estamos agradecidas.
Nuestras madres, mi madre—

¡Qué lindas, qué hermosas!
Que dulces…¡Tan afectuosas!

Unas rosas bellas siempre creciendo con amor;
nos dan abrazos y ternura durante un dolor.
Mi madre, gran persona de belleza y dignidad;
Hay infinito palabras de describirla—y en gran cantidad.

Sonreímos, bailamos y viajamos— allí están;
por nuestro propio bien, nos dan consejos y nos gritan.
Es una linda flor que todos admiran;
Para mi madre y todas las madres queridas—
que dios las bendiga.

UN POEMA PARA QUERIDO PADRE

Dedicado a mi padre, Santiago, la persona más trabajadora que conozco.

Qué bonito es el abrazo de un padre,
sus consejos y apoyo—tan admirable.
Un gran ídolo más allá del horizonte,
trabajando duro y fuerte, sin pidiendo acreditaciones.
Nos enseñan a bailar el vals, manejar un automóvil,
de cómo enfrentar la vida y sonreír—vale por mil.

Es fuerte—un gran trabajador;
mil palabras no sobran pero es mi admirador.
Gritamos, peleamos, sonreímos, lloramos;
en las buenas y las malas.
Pero siempre apoyándome con consejos y muchas palabras.

Es mi padre querido;
y no lo cambio para nadie.
Lo perdono, lo admiro, lo quiero—
si locura de mi parte.
Pero somos sangre de sangre,
y es mi querido padre.

Para todos los padres y mi padre querido—
una gran ovación, un aplauso, un brindis, una linda
celebración.

To Arcadia and Back

Sitting with the family waiting for the flight,
new adventures on arrival and above new heights.
The ticket counters, security point, hot air, long lines—
after all is said and done, we've done this a thousand times.

While passing time before the departure gate,
why not take some pictures as we wait?
The people in the waiting room so diverse from left to right,
including the different airlines from morning to night.

The announcement is made, time to head out to the gate.
It's the moment of takeoff; it's in our fate.

Up in the air with comfort in sight;
takeoff is at bay toward our destination all right.
With the blink of an eye, we arrive on precious land,
as we prance and trolley all hand in hand.

The joys of this beautiful country, the people, food, and sea,
it's as if without a doubt it's all meant to be.
Alas as time goes by, the great music, warm air,
and tropical vibes,
with another blink of an eye it's time to say our good-byes.

And it's back to the airport—so hard to say farewell,
to "la perla del pacífico" and probably back to hell.
But with hopes, this trip has cast a spell on the stressful mind,
and to conquer the waiting obstacles we first left behind.

BEYOND A SHADOW OF A DOUBT

It's the other side of us…
the side that wants to dance and sing and play.
It seems to be hidden,
but always seems to follow.

It's never harmful, but spooks us at times.
Look at it directly and it will never show its face—
      Our truth.

You dance, it dances.
You jump, it jumps.
You leap, it leaps.
A never-ending battle.

      It also seems sad and dark and lonely.

You sit, it sits.
You slouch, it slouches.
You cry and no dear friends, you see no tears from it.
But the stillness it exudes with sad emotions,
as if it were crying with you.

And yet…it will remain with you through happiness and sadness,
anger, and excitement;
Movement and non-movement
and grow old with you, too.

      It's clingy, no doubt about it!!!!

But as clingy as it is, you cannot leave it—
well maybe for darkness.
What can you do, but accept it for what it is—

      Your bona fide self.

HOW ARE YOU DOING?

What's in the question—"how are you doing?"
Don't think you really meant to ask this in passing,
a question just looming.
Are you really interested in the other person's whereabouts;
do you really care if they are happy or just pouts?
Only far and few ever mean to hear the answers
to that very question;
It's better to just say "hi"—fewer selections.
Interesting to see that question thrown so easily in the air;
when in reality the sender, just does not really care.
Would the responder actually take time
to speak details of their day?
The literal answer would be, "Yes, lots to say."
But wouldn't it be easier to simply say hello?
Doesn't mean you are being shallow or just say nothing at all.

Why is that reflexive response thrown around so easily?
If you don't want to make conversation—just let it be.
Perhaps just being courteous or filling in that empty space;
but no need to ask if you don't care; there are other ways.
Hello, how are you doing…how's it going…what's up?
Don't go there, as you might get a response—just stay shut.
But if you truly care, interested, curious or simply inquisitive;
it would be nice to hear how the other person lives.

You may be surprised at the response of deepness and expression;
it could be happiness and glee or anger and depression.
Sometimes that person just needs to let go;
and a simple, "how are you doing?" will let it all show.
You cross each other's path at that very moment for some reason;
winter, spring, summer, fall—it can happen at any season.
Think about that question, next time it's spoken out;
opening Pandora's Box—no doubt.
But being a listening ear at that time of need,
may one day be asked of you to respond to indeed.
In return, that simple question
may turn into a healing experience,
an epiphany of sorts, enlightening moment—a positive influence.

THAT ONE DAY

A moment out in having fun can turn into a day of excitement,
craziness, and madness.
A gathering of friends, chatting, and talking
begins a day of what is yet to come.
>Laughing, strolling, talking, walking—
>what will happen at the end?

Hunger in the mind leads us to a café at the corner.
To sit outside at night, admiring the view of everyone that is
>Laughing, strolling, talking, walking—
>what will happen at the end?

We all then walk around to join others in their strolls while
listening to the thunder in the air.
To our surprise, the rain comes pouring down and we head into a
store for a bargain deal umbrella, but still we're...
>Laughing, strolling, talking, walking—
>this is what we still do until the end.

We strut on down around the streets running into fellas,
winos, quiet alleyways, movie-making streets, and
into the train stations ready to go home, but always...
>Laughing, strolling, talking, walking—
>what will happen at the end?

Running in the station, down escalators and up,
we realize we missed our train!
Well, what else to do, but call for a ride;
it's a moment to improvise.
>As we laugh, stroll, talk, and walk—
>for what is yet to come until the end.

While waiting for our ride, we stand outside on the concrete floor.
Admiring everyone with not a care in the world, ready to explore.
Our help will soon arrive—a father figure, of course.
A simple talk of what went on this one fine day,
while sitting in the car to more laughing and talking and
>finally, yes finally...the end.

 C

Reflections

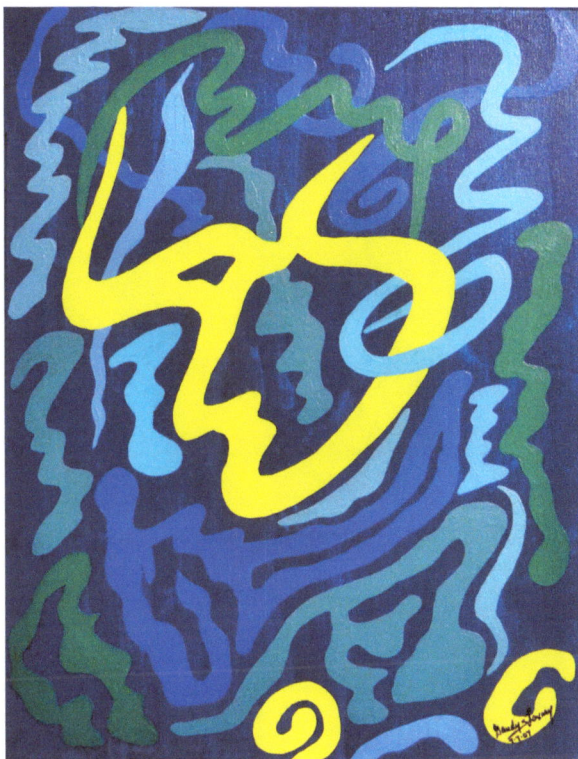

Gaudys Laxury
JUBILEE **(2007)**
Acrylic on Canvas
16 x 20 inches

THE INFINITE LIST

The light...the shadow;
The yin...the yang;
The black...the white;
The love...the hate;
The A to Z;
The tall...the small;
The far...the near;
The mother...the father;
The million to dollar;
The thin...the big;
The donkeys and elephants;
The diamonds...the stones;
The stronger the bones;
The north...the south;
The east to west;
Is there anything left?
The end...no...
            Just the beginning...

Oh, Willow Tree

Frustration is the name of the game,
amidst the dark blue sky and the swaying willow trees.

Running on the open road between the unknown and the unsaid,
beyond the shadows and sublime triangle.

Feeling the waters in the sky like hot steam coming off a radiator,
to the pressures of the volcanic seven summits.

Seeking, looking, gazing at the introspection of the world,
beyond the hourglass—slowly measuring time.

Like Old Father Time and its antiquity to the baby new year,
new hopes and dreams.

One look above beyond bright lights, moonlight thoughts—
the darkness follows, but swallowed by the hollow willow tree.

WHERE ARE YOU?

In the misty gray sky,
up above all around—in and out...
      where are you?

Amongst the brightly lit sky and
traffic lights...
      where are you?

Will we ever meet
and our paths ever cross?
      where are you?

My better half, my soul-mate,
my mirror, my world...
      it's not too late.

Arco iris en el cielo nublado

Que interesante es la vida y
las cosas que nos cruzan en el camino.
Pensando en nada y en nadie,
es el preciso momento donde espontáneo encuentros ocurren.

Una simple conversación, una mirada, una sonrisa—
un momento agradable.
Durante el cielo nublado aparece la claridad.

El intercambio de palabras sin importancia,
pero trayendo alegría por un minuto o dos.
Sin intercambiar nombres, ni saber el pasado, ni el presente,
pero solo esa mirada,
esa sonrisa, esa pequeña conversación—que tranquilidad.

Que interesante es la vida de permitir dos caminos
cruzar por un momento.
De diferente siglos paseando por el mismo peatonal,
pensando en las mismas aspiraciones.

En toda conversación hay un fin—
pocas palabras que hasta el sol aparece en medio de la oscuridad.
Positivo inspiración, respiración, admiración…
para seguir adelante en este camino del arco iris en reflexión.

LIFE'S UNEXPLAINABLES

Sometimes life presents you with different facets
that are unexplainable.
The tragedies of life cannot be explained,
but only in one moment all this comes to an end.

Throughout life, we see so many different things,
so many things that we wish we could have changed—
ourselves, others, life…

Life comes and goes, like the sands of time
looking through the hourglass;
that on one day's notice you wish to turn
upside down and all around.
One moment or the other
you'll have a second chance to make things right,
but then you wonder just why things happen the way they did.

Life's creation, life's pleasures,
through and through, it's the unexplainable.

Is it Mother Nature, Mother Destiny, or some outer limits in time
that cannot be explained;
but unbeknownst to the world,
it comes and goes like the hands of time?

Through it all you wish to scream and yell up at the sky;
say why, oh why did it happen this way,
why couldn't it turn out a different way?

      The unexplainable.

The things that just happen, with the blink of an eye,
a curve ball in time—life's unexplainable.

PENSANDO EN LAS HORAS

Son tantos los pensamientos del día
que las horas pasan y todavía hay más que reflexionar.

Reflexiones en un espejo de quien será y
no pensando en el que dirán.
Dirigiendo una palabra en ese aire frío,
para entender y suavizar la locura de la mente.

Una mentalidad casi absurda, lleno de pensamientos e ideas,
como un crucigrama, difícil de entender.
Comprenderse, motivarse y aceptarse es la realidad,
que un día tiene veinticuatro horas.

Horas que vienen y van como las aguas turbulentas,
y tratando de organizar el día—nadando suavemente
a través de las corrientes.

Las horas pasan, pero la tranquilidad continua, con un
respiro profundo hasta el día siguiente.

ISSUES IN OUR LIVES

So many different ideas clustered around one mind.
A variety of problems ranging from black to white.
So many causes to focus on, so many issues to be seen.
Bring our minds together and our thoughts so clean.

Issues in our lives, problems come and go.
Running all through time and walking with the flow.
Expectations to yearn for and ideas heard throughout time.
Each day we come together, thoughts, one of a kind.

Although we have these problems and issues that arise.
Many thoughts and ideas also cross our minds.
To find solutions and ideas to be made,
to solve the issues in our lives and ideas to be paid.

We still go on each day in life to try and solve
the problems in our lives so loud and quite involved.
To solve the problems, we must listen to our voices so clear;
and expand our ideas for all of us to hear.

DESTINY

Anger's in my mind, confusion's in the air;
can't wait for Mother Destiny to show me the light.
Growing all through life, learning along the way,
from everyone, everything, and day by day.

> Striving, growing, learning, falling—
> picking yourself up and keep on walking.

Walking every day with no way turning back,
continuing to search for answers to unpack.
Finding yourself out,
asking all the right questions,
for your being here is human nature.

> Striving, growing, learning, falling—
> picking yourself up and keep on walking.

Waiting for a signal, looking for a sign,
listening for a moment to stand up with open eyes.
Choosing many paths, if there's any one to choose from;
brings a strain of incomprehension to the soul.

> Striving, growing, learning, falling—
> picking yourself up and keep on walking.

Something meant for you and me and everyone around.
Patience is what is needed, breathe in each day.
Amongst all things in life of what is said and done.
To choose your path and fight, one should be...

> Striving, growing, learning, falling—
> picking yourself up and keep on walking.

80

ALBATROSS LOVE

Gaudys Laxury
AMOR DE ALBATROSS (2015)
Oil on Canvas
12 x 24 inches

CR ═══════════════════════════════

PURSUIT OF SOMETHING

Don't say…
I will call you, when you don't.
I will text you, when you won't.
I will pass by to see you…just from afar.
We'll talk later…cross my heart.
Great things will happen to you…just not with me.
I will reach you when I get back;
couldn't get to you, I busted my knee.
You're cute…but not sexy.
You're amazing…but next, please.
You're nice…but not bad.
You're bad and not nice enough…don't get mad.
You're too tall…I can't see the sky.
You're too short…I see that cutie over you passing by.
You're complicated…simplicity would be sweeter.
You're sweet and simple…complexity is not bitter.
You're mysterious…you must be a spy.
You're outspoken…no mystery—bye–bye!
Today you brighten my day…but tomorrow reality will kick in.
You make me feel so much better…yet the feeling
is not so genuine.
I'm concentrating on my studies…I'm just not into you.
I'm focused on my career…you're just not a part
of the long-term view.
A contradiction of endless anomalies
in the pursuit of something,
better to say more or shhh…don't say nothing.

NEXT

Frustration is what is felt when there is no communication.
You give a brother one chance,
forgive and forget at second glance.

But then the third time around,
you just don't know what to do.
Time to breathe, time to scream,
but better yet laugh it off and go on to the next.

Emancipation, freedom from this long-lasting relation.
Don't know how he works his game,
you give it your all and don't get the same.

Holidays have come and gone,
and no phone calls all season long.
Time to breathe, time to scream,
but better yet laugh it off and go on to the next.

Explanation…no need for that,
too little of this and too much spat.
What's the point of nonsense words?
Heard it the first time, second, and third.

Words fly in and out of time;
it's better to listen, then to rewind
and move onto better things, so…

Time to breathe, time to scream, but better yet laugh it off—
and go on to the next.

Go on to the next, the next best thing.
There's plenty for everyone and the world to bring.
One for each of us in life, so breathe and scream;
but better yet laugh it off and go on to the next…

the next big dream.

SEARCHING THROUGH LIFE

On to find someone at this time is just so difficult.
Running all through life, running against the wind.
Trying to figure out who's meant for you
when they will appear—your special boo.

Breathing, breathing is what we should do.
Hoping, hoping for life to come through.
Just wait a while and all will come true.

To walk around with no one to hear.
Doing things without no fear.
Thinking about those moments
of being around that special someone,
but realizing that someone is just the wind.

The day will come when that someone will appear.
Just close your eyes and something will be near.
You feel a touch, no longer is the wind,
but someone to walk with you through life—your kindred.

ONE MORE ENCOUNTER

So many years have come and gone;
so many days go by and by.
But still I think of you today,
even though we've hung out a couple of times.

The look in your eyes, the smile on your face,
made my heart beat faster every day.

I only wish we had the chance,
I only wish we had those years,
to see that look, that smile next to me and for a while.

I didn't think our last encounter would be the end,
for that explains how my heart just didn't mend.

Only hope our paths will cross once again,
to say to you how I feel and what could have been.
Only hope you're still alive,
not in the sky—way up high.

For just one moment, just one time,
to tell you where we could go forever
and finish the rest of this time together.

UNFORGOTTEN IMAGE

You've always crossed my mind when I turn and
look at everything.
I think of you in every way.
An image of your face, I see day by day.

Found it hard to let go sometimes
of all the days and years we've spent together.
The way it could have been, happiness you see—
where things were better.

I'm crazy…my love;
just seeing you as peaceful as a white dove.
Together we learned so many things;
but it was all ending—broken wings.

How could this be?

I still see your image in everything.
The laughter, tears, heartbreak it brings.
It was all just a matter of time for all of that to end;
but still I see your unforgotten image—
my sweetheart and friend.

TRUST

Trust is a key that can't be open to just anyone.
Talking to many people all lifelong.
Looking into eyes, but seeing all the emptiness inside.
Trying to find out who's real and who's not…find out.

Trusting you, trusting me.
Feeling you, feeling me.
Finding you, finding me.

Asking many questions in my mind.
A clouded judgment in front of me;
but opening my eyes to find the truth—that's the key.

Reading in between the lines of what is said,
while people cross my path, come and go as they please,
always trust in those who ask no questions or tease.

To trust, to feel, to find…
is the key that can't be open to just anyone.

DYING TO BE FREE

Dying to be free from the emptiness inside of me.
Something is in the air and in the autumn breeze.
Walking in hopes and feelings to admire.
Kissing with our lips so soft and full of desire.

Growing all inside and stirrings in the soul.
Floating in the sea, in the ocean...silky air.
Wanting you so badly, but walking against the wind.
Round and round we go—
you just don't talk to me.

Communicate to me, listen to me.
Anger's in my mind when you don't open up to me.
Words fly in the air and there's silence tonight.
Dying to be free—
you just don't talk to me.

Oh! Dying to be free...
Oh! Those feelings so deep.
Free from emptiness that is felt from you to me.
Free from loneliness while you're turning the key.

INNER PEACE

Gaudys Laxury
BALANCE (2015)
Oil on Canvas
20 x 24 inches

BLACK MAMBA
Poem dedicated to domestic violence victims

A graceful, but skittish Dendroaspis,
which aims when provoked with a venomous kiss.
Aggression in the eyes of the mamba,
it aims quick and direct as it dances to the samba.

This unpredictable serpent of great agility,
can strike without a moment's notice with great capability.
A bad tempered diurnal and ambush predator,
an unparalleled match to that of a matador.

A hunter in its own right,
can bring down its prey within its sight.
An attacker of unparalleled ferocity,
a mover, a shaker, of high velocity.

Avoiding confrontation one moment and tranquil the next,
walking down the semi-dry savannah until the kiss of death.
That silent moment when dryness is in the air;
seeking to quench its thirst without a care.

All calm and pleasant as days go by,
hiding under rock crevices, waiting for its victim—
       the innocent passerby.

The roller coaster emotions stirring once again;
crawling, slithering, and sliding—
       beware the mamba strikes again.

HEARTACHE

Feeling so out of place…out of mind, body, and soul;
too young to roll in the big leagues,
too old to play with dolls.
More than a quarter of a century has passed;
along with the drama and heartache—
an improvisational thespian cast.

The frustration of not moving forward…go, go, go!
Always feeling like it's in reverse—it truly blows!

Six months have passed, a year, two, three, four…
well, we get the point;
but no one tells you that time flies so fast,
no advisement, not even a checkpoint.

No, this is not your typical inspirational poetry,
but an ode to the cymbaltic;
a moment for venting, screaming, shouting,
and all that dark logic.

Save the hugs, the faith, the prayers as life is at a standstill;
nothing seems to be progressing,
it's an unbelievable downhill.

And then there is that
"to hang out with anyone, just to hangout" mentality,
but when deep down inside you're yearning for stability.

What is age, but an idiotic definition of time?
A sublime stupidity— an excuse to contest a long, hard climb?

THE DESERT SPHINX

Walking in the middle of the Sahara Desert,
without a sight on the horizon.
Drinking but only the drips seen upon
layers and layers of silky sweat.
Thinking of where to go and which direction to take,
but still walking in this lonely desert.

      The sun—

so hot and humid hits the skin
like a nice summer's day at the lovely beach;
but take away the ocean, the sand, and the people at hand.
Wondering which path to take, which road to follow;
as if there is anything left to swallow.

      Run, run!!

Nowhere to hide in this lonely desert,
but only your thoughts and dreams and
wishes will lead the path.
A stroll, a leap, a skip…a jump…
but move forward as your mind is the companion
in this riddle—the lovely riddle of the Sphinx.

SNOW-STORMY THINKING

A snowy atmosphere and cold but tranquil day,
peaceful skies, melancholic moments come our way.

A day filled with shoveling snow, salt ice, and traveling woes—
but also hot soups, snow angels, and
not walking on ice on your tippy toes.

This pleasant scene of blankets of white
makes you want to think—will it be the same at night?

But come nightfall as you fall asleep,
the snow will wait for you—probably 12 inches deep.

This sea of white is nothing to despair
because sooner than you know it, spring is in the air.

MIXED WORLD

One day you realize you're surrounded
by all different types of people.
Different personalities, laughs, expressions, and attitudes.
Through and through you find yourself
being one of those mixed colors.

Crazy world, filled with voices to be heard.
Crazy world, mixed with characters that grow.

A rainbow of different colors, a shadow beyond a doubt.
Of different moods and strange beings,
that one moment you find yourself a part of—it's worth seeing.

Expressions of confusion, expressions of demand—
of madness, sadness, happiness, and commands.
One second you're talking, another you're not.
Each day is different; each moment is shot.

But realizing you're in this crazy world
full of differences and shadows.
Makes you think that you're not excluded
from this crazy, mixed world.

CRYSTAL TIME

Heartbreaks, confusion, frustration
are things that happen in life.
As time goes by, we stand up and
confront those extremes in life.

Wanting but wasting every precious moment in life,
creating those things that we don't want to exist,
but growing, throwing, living, and loving.

Time and time again, you feel like good things have happened;
but each step you take forward—somewhere, somehow,
something pulls you back.

A teardrop is needed from up high and above,
looking at that crystal time and
seeing yourself as life goes by.

Finding yourself walking in and out of life
and through the open windows of this world
to see the opportunities that are sought.

Every inch you take and every moment you seek,
you've wandered in life with all confusions aside
as you peer through that crystal time.

WANDERING EYES

This is a crazy world, mixed up with rainbow colors,
hardly black and white.
Walking into a room full of different
personalities and mysteries.
Wanting to not be bothered and just living life day by day.
Needing to leave the room as quick as the flash of a light.

Wanting to zip in and out of every moment each day,
without having everyone in your business—
get out of the way.
Being able to breathe and break
from all those wandering eyes.
To stroll and walk as quick as the air,
to do your thing without those passerby.

To just be one of those everyday people,
not wanting to be bothered.
In the mood for a solo stroll, but feeling those eyes—
being followed.

To take a few steps and feel the motion of the body and
obstacles of life surround your everyday mood.
Questioning your every step—

Really? How rude.

But the answer to them wandering eyes,
is to breathe, stroll, and do your thing...
be different and unique.

Break from every moment, all the darkness, all the glances;
break from all the curious eyes, talks, and madness.

CRYPTIC CONUNDRUM

Gaudys Laxury
CONFUSION **(2007)**
Acrylic on Canvas
16 x 20 inches

TO WHISTLE OR NOT

A movement of the lips,
an expression of a bird like sound.
The announcement of being present,
a pleasant sound for all around.

The way to connect your subconscious mind to the world,
to release the tensions of the day, the hour, the minute.
Pleasant tunes behind thin walls,
just whistle away, the sky's the limit.

Expecting that whistle at a particular time of the day,
where is Mr. Whistler, whistling away?
No way of hearing that beautiful sound,
unless the mind's attuned and ears abound.

But where is that whistle heard like clockwork—
tick-tick-tickin' away?
The mysterious sound, all around, up and down,
bouncing off walls—it's here to stay.

DROP OF WATER

Living life day by day, inch by inch, time by time,
for in each moment, the thin brisk air brings it in.
Expect surprises to happen at any time
and when it arises it's a moment of gleeful tearfulness.

A drop of water in the lens of time
is all that's needed to feel free and alive.
Just one answer is needed; one word to clear your mind.
As you walk amidst the clear blue sky to find the answer.

Walking all around in complete confusion,
not knowing right from wrong.
Not understanding what's next in store and
wishing that it all makes sense.

A test of life results in sweet sorrows of mixed confusion,
not knowing what's in store in the end.
Maybe one day it will come to a closure as we keep walking
toward that drop of water falling on the lens.

MYSTERY

One day you come across an alley, pondering the meaning of life
and some wino appears asking—what's up?—
thankfully without a knife.

Hey, man, I just don't understand…"what life's all about?"
"Don't worry," he says, just take it in stride and walk on by.
Just look at me and you will see that life's a great big mystery.

      Hey *la*…hey *la la la*…life's a great big mystery.
      Just take it all in and you will see.

So I nod my head and gave him a dime;
before understanding the meaning of life,
it's all just a matter of time.

I walk inside a park with four strangers along the way…
singing their doo-wops of life with a cool sway.
Hey, y'all, what's going on?
We're just singing the la di das on this park's lawn…

So what y'all think of life itself?
Just look at us and you will see;
to smile and breathe and sing in glee.

      Hey *la*…hey *la la la*…life's a great big mystery.
      Just take it all in and you will see.

Saw it all along the streets and in the air,
I ask my questions with all to share. And one thing I noticed is to
hear and see, to chill and listen and feel in glee.

Of the goodness of life of just being here,
among all things it should be clear.
That life's a great big mystery,
but take it all in and you will see.

CONFUSED

Confusion is a part of life,
deep inside the mind, body, and soul.
Touching all the things that we don't know,
the things in life that confuse us—
an empty hole.

Questioning all things—finding our niche,
asking what's our life purpose.
Digging through the black darkness and what's on the surface.

Confusion is a part of life,
in the mind, body, and soul.
Questioning all the things that we don't know,
the things in life that confuse us through our soul.

FIGURING OUT

Figuring out what to do at this time and
seeing everything through frenzied eyes,
you might just come across some lies.

Figuring out all the questions and
truth until you see the light—
keep talking and asking questions with force and might.

Figuring out the answers by walking down that tunnel—
seeking answers with a message to send,
and taking that path will lead you to the end.

Figure it out.

ANGEL LIFE

Strolling, strolling, strolling…
going one step forward and taking one step back.
Doing all the things that come to mind and
through the lens of life.

Walking down the alleys and strolling down the block.
Showing all the moves that we all got.
The beach is to the left, the shadows to the right,
we just can't seem to see the outcomes
even with a passing light.

Loving the angels of my life, growing with the times.
Loving the freshness of nature and open vines.

It's half past nine and friends are grooving to the night.
Clear as the air, tranquil as the sea, calm as the wind.
Seeing different people crossing our lives.

Loving the angels in my life, growing with the times.
Loving the universe of life and all the clear signs.

UN PEQUEÑO DESEO PARA EL AÑO NUEVO

Abriendo la ventana en este mes de enero—tan frío,
tratando de pensar en grandes metas—hay dios mío.

Pensando en amores de todas clase esta vez,
y cuando va a pasar—esperamos el siguiente mes.

Y si nada el próximo mes pues vemos hasta noviembre,
para que vengan los amores en tiempo de fiestas en diciembre.

Y con respecto a las metas respiramos profundamente,
que se lleguen a cumplir suavecito y alegremente.

Y por si en caso no se cumplen en este año venidero,
no se den por vencidos que algún día lo alcancemos.

END ON A HIGH NOTE

Gaudys Laxury
CHARDI KALA (2015)
Oil on Canvas
20 x 24 inches

CR

COLORS

Colors, colors—a rainbow effect,
yellow, blue, red, orange, aquamarine,
so many color palettes.
Why not coquelicot, deep koamaru, or dark tangerine?

All those colors with bright lights,
all seen at great heights.
Nothing dull or dark, gray or black;
the louder, the better, don't get taken aback.

An eccentric individual dressing up for life,
free as a bird, cut that chain with a knife.
A colorful being, one color is not enough;
slap it on and go, life is a canvas—not all tough.

Seeing life through rainbow colors is a great sight;
each color in the spectrum is like the moon and sun— so bright.
Don't get me wrong—
the mauve, olives, grays and blacks are also keen;
for those sophisticated moments, a sight unseen.

But jazz it up with electric blue;
and if feeling sexy and bold, slap on red, too.
Creative thoughts flowing like the currents out at sea;
it's all due to those magical colors bringing us joy and glee.

GLEEFUL MOMENT

The stop of time.
The silence in the air.
The millimeter of a second.
The moment of ultimate glee.

When accomplishment is attained.
All hands on deck.
Keep that eye on the prize.
The moment to yell—yay me!!!

A pat on the back.
A hug to oneself.
A high five of sort.
Never to abort.

Perseverance.
Perspiration.
Dedication.
All in moderation.

A skip and a hop.
The drumroll, the base.
A back-flip, a front flip—flippity, flop.
Swaying and singing—wop ba da bebop!!

LINDA ROSA
Palabras de mi padre a mi querida madre.

Tu eres en mi vida la mas linda rosa,
la mas linda cosa de mi realidad.

Te quiero mi vida por que eres mi todo,
en este momento de mi realidad.

Te llevo adentro en mi corazon.
Le pido al cielo por tu vida y esplendor,
y me arrodillo antes de ti mi amor.

Tu eres en mi vida la mas linda rosa,
la mas linda cosa de mi realidad.

Te quiero mi vida, por que eres mi todo,
en este momento de mi realidad.

HEARTBEAT GOES—*THUMP! THUMP!*

Listen to the beat of the music in the air—

> *Thump! Thump!*

Rain comes pouring down against the hard glass window,
the ringing of the phone, and the rapping of the blinds—

> *Thump!*

Your mind starts racing to the sounds and
the beating of the drums.
With the ringing of the doorbell and your sweetie by your side,
you listen to the rhythms in the air and the sounds of the night.

It's a Wednesday night,
the middle of the week with nothing to do.
The next thing you know you're in the city.
The sky is dark, the stars are out;
you and everyone are roaming around.

Feel the beat in the air;
everyone *thumps, thumps* before deciding what is yet to come.
The sounds of the night and what's in our souls,
decisions to be made for the night is young.

Finally—as we walk through the night and into alley ways,
we come across a small jazz joint to fulfill our…

> *Thump! Thumps!*

feelings of heartbeats just jump.

AHH...THE CITY

Oh, the bright lights and big city that never sleeps,
where they walk, talk, hustle and bustle...all laughs and weeps.

The sun goes down and the lights turn up.
The music's blaring; the sirens sound...a skip and a hop.

It's a fast-paced life,
   no time to unwind, no time to breathe,
   no time to sleep...it's all too deep.

The year comes to an end, what madness as time flies by;
leave the past behind,
   the aches and pains aside...just say good-bye.

Still the city with its fast pace, bright lights, and high beams,
ring in the new year with new hopes and big dreams.

BEAT OF THE NIGHT

The stars beyond the horizon glow dim throughout the night;
but out of darkness lurks the luminescent deep and bright light.
Thoughts come in and out with the beat of every sound;
the pouncing, the movement, the thumping...
ready to be unwound.

The night is dark, the unconditional shallow halls, and
quiet alleyways;
but then comes the music, the people, and
the heartbeats that go on for days.

Thump, thump, thump...boom da da da da boom;
an explosion of lights, sounds, people—
it's one of those crazy deep tunes.

Let's go paint that ceiling with rhythmic pleasantry,
for it's a night of fun and laughter—the perfect zen and glee.

NIGHTLIFE

Going out into the nightlife, seeing bright lights, and
everyone all around.
Crazy world, loud, real music, bodies dancing, beats all down and
all around...
      Round and round.

Shaking is the best thing to do.
Body to body, drinking and drinking.
      Round and round...all around.
      Mingling, driving free, just you and me and everyone—
      all around.

Going out into the nightlife, seeing bright lights, and
everyone all around.
The night is young, but yet has ended to stop and think;
it's a memory.

It's time to close your eyes and sleep.
To rest and dream of everything that's all around.
      Of mingling, driving free, just you and me and every
      one—all around.

But yet there's always still tomorrow...
A brand new day into the nightlife, seeing bright lights,
and everyone all around.

      Of mingling, driving free, just you and me and every
      one—all around, all around...round and round...

GROOVING

Grooving, grooving, grooving way up high.
Shaking your booty, booty, booty from the bottom to the top.
Electrifying moves all night long,
lights are glowing off your body and soul.

Grooving, grooving, grooving all night long.
To the rhythm of the night, each body tonight,
showing off is nice.

Sweating bodies through smoky air,
loud, loud music running through our souls.
Moving rhythm at one full glance,
close them eyes and feel the music in the air.

It's half past five, but keep on grooving.
The world is yours, when the rhythm's all there.
Keep shaking and moving all night long.
It's your dance floor and no one cares.

TRA LA LA THOUGHTS

La di da, la di da—da da da da…
Sweet, sweet world!
Driving down the alleyway, got no place to stay, but hey…
        Tra la la today.

Gather your friends tonight and waiting for that little sign
into the ins and outs of life.

Flying high, flying low.
Spirits alive and *tra la la* tonight.

Figuring out the plan tonight.
Music echoing in the air,
with your bodies moving to the sound
and all still…
        Tra la la today.

Moving along with no time or thoughts by your side.
You all just stroll along at night.
Till the break of dawn with just one thought of…

Flying high, flying low, with spirits alive, and
la di das…tra la las of the day.

GOOD TIMES

Have a little laughter and party up with music;
have a little fun and some innocent, good time.
A great big day and night to not get sick,
perfect moment to celebrate with champagne and wine.

Hang out throughout the hours of the night,
forget about all the things in the long, hardworking day.
Show a little laughter and the pearly white;
it's a great day and night for us all to play.

To dance with all your friends in celebration of the night and
forget about the aches and pain.
It's the middle of the night and have a good time,
even in the rain.

Walking through the streets among the sad-looking people,
forget about the problems, all the sorrows and the pain.
Keep walking and dancing to that fever and
just listen to those beats running through your vein.

Have a great big laugh and top it off with music;
dance it off, go play, it's your night.
Music...dancing...great moments;
it's the time to shine and be bright.

ℭ℞

ABOUT THE AUTHOR

Gaudys Laxury paints and writes. The two blessings seldom visit her simultaneously but always spontaneously.

Gaudys has been writing poems and painting since her early teen years. With *The Pearl inside the Orchid*, she found the courage to step outside of the box and present her innermost thoughts and emotions over the decades out to the world. The poems were written during each stage of her life, from elementary school to adolescent times, coming of age to her young adult and professional life...images and words came to mind while capturing the world.

Through the ups, downs, zigzags, crisscross, and obstacles presented along the way, she has coasted through the waves and hopes that readers can relate to at least one of the poems or find inspiration through the paintings.

A self-taught artist with an analytical mind and a creative spin, Gaudys has combined words and images to connect on a deeper level. She studied politics, law, and communications during her graduate years, while always maintaining her passions in the arts.

Writing and art keep her balanced and allows her to express her most intimate thoughts, creating zen in tumultuous moments.

Gaudys lives in New York City and is of Ecuadorian descent. She has an art website, www.glaxarts.com, and can be found lurking around the treasure troves of the Big Apple or traveling to quench her inquisitive nature; marching to the beat of her own drum—seeking inspiration and truth.

www.ingramcontent.com/pod-product-compliance
Lightning Source LLC
Chambersburg PA
CBHW051233090426
42740CB00001B/5